Lessons with Geoff Thompson

The Ground Fighting Series

Volume Four

Arm bars and locks

Other books and videos by Geoff Thompson:

Watch My Back - A Bouncer's Story.
Bouncer (the sequel to Watch My Back).
The Pavement Arena - adapting combat martial arts to the street.
Real Self Defence.
Real Grappling.
Real Punching
Real Kicking.
Weight Training - For the Martial Artist.
Animal Day - Pressure testing the Martial Arts.
Tuxedo Warrior - Tales of a Mancunian Bouncer. By Cliff Twemlow. Foreword By Geoff Thompson.
Fear - The Friend of Exceptional People (Techniques in controlling fear)
Dead or Alive - The complete self protection hand book. (As released by Paladin Press in the USA.)

The Ground Fighting series:

Vol One - Pins, The Bedrock
Vol Two - Escapes.
Vol Three - Chokes and Strangles.
Vol Five - Fighting from your knees.
Vol Six - Fighting from your back.

Videos - (all videos approx. one hr.):

Lessons with Geoff Thompson
Animal Day - Pressure testing the martial arts.
Animal Day part 2, A deeper look - The fights.
Three Second Fighter - The sniper option.
The Ground Fighting series:
Vol One - Pins, the bedrock.
Vol Two - Escapes.
Vol Three - Chokes and strangles
Vol Four - Bars and joint locks.
Vol Five - Fighting from your knees.
Vol Six - Fighting from your back.

Forthcoming books:

Real Head, Knees and Elbows.
Contemporary Self Protection (released as Dead or Alive in USA)
Blue Blood on the Mat - Athol Oakley - Foreword Geoff Thompson.
On the Door - Further Bouncer Adventures.

Copyright © Geoff Thompson 1996

All rights reserved

No part of this book may be reproduced by any means, nor transmitted, nor translated into a machine language without the written permission of the publisher.

Summersdale Publishers
PO Box 49
Chichester
West Sussex
PO19 2FJ
United Kingdom

A CIP catalogue record is available for this book from the British Library.

ISBN 1 873475 81 0

Photographs by Paul Raynor (01484 451115)

ABOUT THE AUTHOR

Geoff Thompson was a doorman for 9 years and has been a practising martial artist for over 20 years. He presently holds a 4th Dan C.E.K.A., 4th Dan B.C.A., 2nd Dan K.U.G.B., 1st Dan Modga Kung Fu, A.B.A. Ass. Boxing Coach, Amateur Wrestling Coach and a B.T.K.B.C. Muay Thai Boxing Coach. Geoff is a former British Weapons Champion and has also trained widely in Aikido, Judo and is qualified to teach Ju-Jitsu. He has frequently appeared on national and international television and radio talking about and giving advice on self protection and related subjects. He is currently the B.B.C. T.V. Good Morning self defence expert. Geoff's first book, Watch My Back - A Bouncer's Story, is fast becoming a cult book. His other books have also been hugely successful. He has been published and commissioned by many publications including G.Q. Magazine, and has written 12 television plays based on his Bouncer books. Geoff is recognised as an international authority on the art of self protection.

Ground Fighting: Volume Four

Note: With ground fighting techniques the author recommends that you practice only under supervision to avoid accidents and always employ the 'tap system' in practice (if you want to submit or a technique is too painful or you wish to stop practice at any time tap the mat, tap yourself or your opponent with your hand or foot; if this is not possible just say to your opponent 'tap'). If an opponent taps out it is imperative that you release your hold immediately or suffer the consequence of what might be serious injury, and remember, what goes around comes around. If you do not release when he taps he may not release the next time you tap.

Important note
If you have or believe you have a medical condition, the techniques outlined in this book should not be attempted without first consulting your doctor. The authors and the publishers cannot accept any responsibility for any proceedings or prosecutions brought or instituted against any person or body as a result of the use or misuse of techniques described in this book or any loss, injury or damage caused thereby.

ACKNOWLEDGEMENTS

With special thanks to Marc McFann and my good friend and grappling sempai Rick Young.

Arm Bars and Locks

Contents

Introduction — 14

Bars and Joint locks from:

Chapter one   From the Mount Position.   21

Chapter two   From the scarf hold.   36

Chapter three From the upper 4 1/4 hold down.   48

Chapter four   From the side 4 1/4 hold down.   61

Chapter five   From the opponent's scissor guard.   72

Chapter six   Finishing from Juji Gatame.   85

Chapter seven Drilling   91

Conclusion   97

Ground Fighting: Volume Four

Review

For those that have read the previous volumes of this series I apologise for repeating material. I would like to, before I start talking about Bars and locks from the various positions, quickly review the basic pins, because if you do not know them a lot of the speak through out the text may seem like gobble-de-gook.

I have no intention of actually going into the histrionics of the holds, how to defend them and attack from them and the real intricacies etc etc etc. that, as I said, is a volume on its own.
I will repeat though that the pins are the bedrock of ground fighting and to go on to finishing techniques of a complex nature before learning the imperative basics is a quick way to failing at everything that you attempt.

Master the standing and walking before you try the running and sprinting, the control of the opponent on the floor, via the pinning techniques, is so very, very, VERY important that to miss it is, metaphorically, like diving in the water before you have learned to swim. All I will list in this chapter is the holds themself with one accompanying illustration so that, if you haven't read the other books and have no knowledge of the 'ground' you'll at least understand the 'speak'.

The Mount Position:
Side Mount; Reverse Mount

Ground Fighting: Volume Four

Arm Bars and Locks

The Side Four Quarter

Ground Fighting: Volume Four

The Scarf Hold

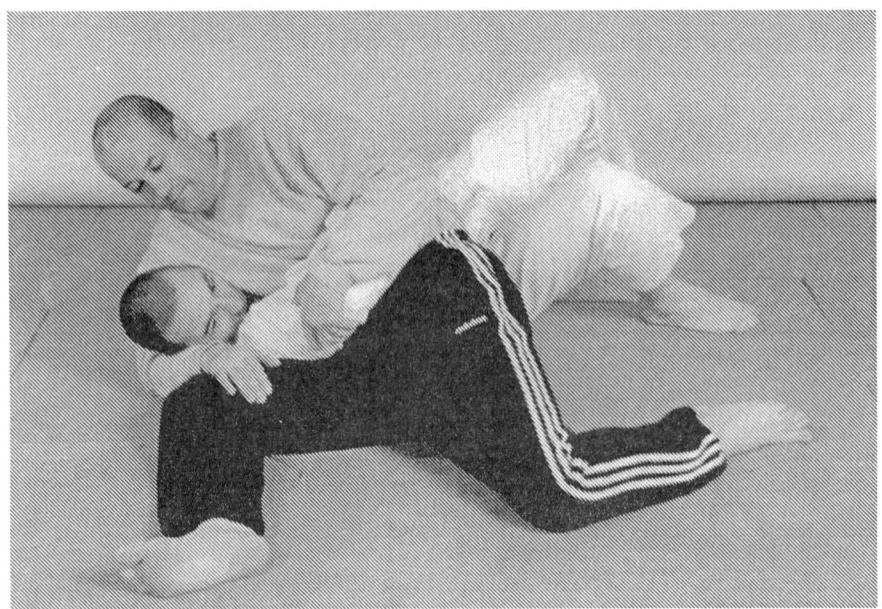

The Jack-Knife

Arm Bars and Locks

Reverse Scarf Hold

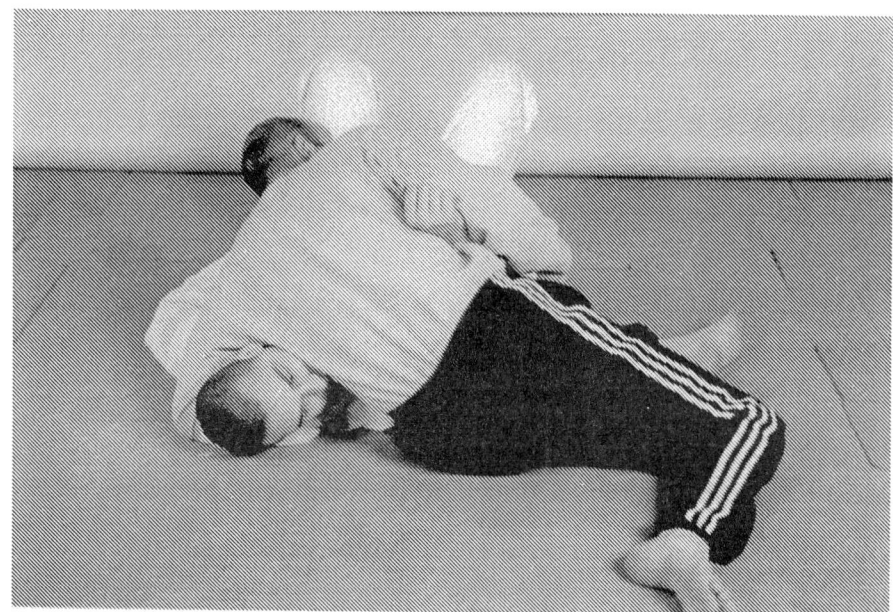

Upper 4 /14 Pin

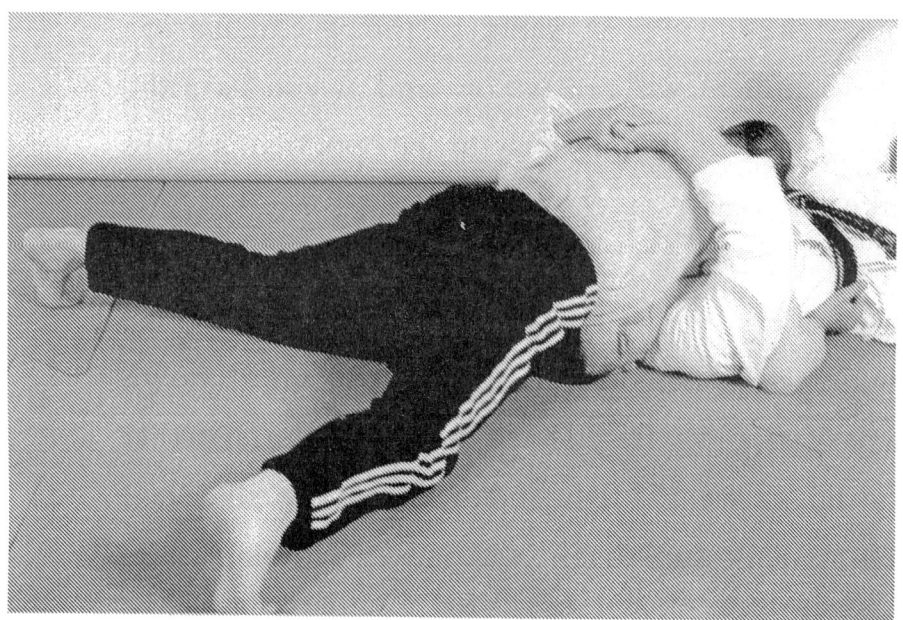

Ground Fighting: Volume Four

Introduction

Many people underestimate the potency of the bars and locks, mostly because they have only seen and not felt them in the controlled arena or contest arena. Certainly from a spectators point of view, the arm bar goes on and the opponent taps out - and that's about the end of it. In reality, on the pavement arena the opponent will not tap out and, if you have the desire you can literally snap of the opponent's limbs like twigs.

One of my friends in Coventry, a renowned Judoka was once cornered by an unsuspecting youth down a dark alley. My friend had already told the chap that he did not want to fight and then tried to walk away, his assailant, sure that he was on to a winner because

Arm Bars and Locks

my friend refused to fight, gave chase and tried to force the issue. Seconds later he had a broken leg and two broken arms. This is the prowess of the Kansetsu-waza (Joint locks). I'd be lying if I told you that many of the joint locks are advanced ground fighting techniques that will need many hours of flight time to perfect, but that's OK, we don't really want them to be easy to learn otherwise everyone will be good at them.

That's what I really like about the ground fighting in general, it is so physically and mentally demanding that only a very small percentage of those that start the journey into the labyrinths of the ground will actually finish the journey. Most will stop and turn back at the very first hurdle, those that do stay the course and acquire the knowledge therefore will be special people. The knowledge only really goes to those that pay the price, in the world of real the price can be very high but the final product will be a polished and empirical vehicle that will ride high and proud on the roads of contemporary violence.

It is my opinion that the veteran ground fighter is potentate amongst the melée of other combatants, that is not to say that I do not rate other forms of fighting, it is just that I have practised many and the most demanding and yet satisfying of them all, the one that gave me the most confidence when reality reared its ugly head was the ground fighting. We have a paradox here because, whilst I sit here at the computer, cup of tea in hand (just finished a couple of toasted tea cakes, actually) telling you off the prowess of the ground fighter and my love for the ground fighting arts I know that, should a fight kick off when I nip into the city to day it will be the punching range that I seek and 95 % of the time that is where I will finish the altercation, usually with my opponent unconscious. Even though the ground is where most fights end up, it is not where they start, they start at conversation range, which is punching range.

If you can maintain this range with the use of a fence (see 3 second fighter book/video) and attack the attacker from there with a pre-emptive strike (working on the premise that you have already lost the option of flight and cannot verbally defuse the situation) the fight will end, clinically, and usually

Arm Bars and Locks

in seconds, from where it started. Unfortunately most people do not operate from a fence and they will not, for whatever reason, become pre-emptive so the fight usually always goes through vertical grappling and hits the ground in a hurry. This is when (and why) the ground fighting knowledge is a God send.

Whilst this may all seem peripheral to what we are teaching within this series it is not, it is the ground fighting knowledge that allows me the confidence to commit my attacks from the vertical range. Many people do not completely commit their attacks because they are worried about getting grabbed and going to ground (because they are ill prepared) so they under commit and are chased and grabbed anyway and, et voila - you're in grappling range.

Other fighters, the over confident ones that believe they are too good at their own range to be taken to the floor, so don't practice ground fighting for this reason. They either over commit their techniques believing that they cannot fail, or freeze when the opponent smacks them in the teeth and they realise that reality is not a Jacky Chan Movie (no disrespect

Jackie) rather it is a mouth full of blood and a monster that can cure constipation and doesn't give a monkeys **ck how many dans you hold, or how many punches you can throw in one second, or how many competitions you have won. He also ends up on the deck with the teeth of adversity biting his nose from his face. And a road digger from hell with ten pints of larger and three E's in him will give anyone of any standard the hardest five minutes of their life if they are not switched on.

The untrained fighter is the most unpredictable fighter on the planet, he will not fight to a pattern and will not respond to many of the tricks that work against the indoctrinated gym fighter, he will wear the broken nose you give him like a badge of battle- and still carry on, and if he beats you he will beat you bad, literally kicking you in the head until some one steps forward to stop him or he stops from sheer exhaustion. So when we fight the monster on the street we have to be a bigger animal than he, and we need to know techniques that will and can destroy if we want them to. The saddest people that I have met are people that say 'Oh no, I wouldn't use that

Arm Bars and Locks

technique' as though biting or butting are below them, these are the people that are going to really struggle when the shit hits the fan because they are so ill prepared and so out of date that they will be blasted off the planet by an enemy that will hit them so hard with their own morality that they will go back in time and when they wake up their clothes will be out of fashion, but at least then their clothes might match their concepts.

Sorry, I went off on a tangent there, but, many of the techniques in this series are as brutal as they are immediate - ignore them at your own peril.

Just to reiterate, although these techniques are a little complex at times stick with them and work them hard, eventually they will not seem difficult. Rather they will seem not easy but obvious and will get you out of many a difficult situation. As with the chokes and strangles in the last volume of this series the bars and locks can be used either to control or to destroy, when the lock is secured the choice, as they say, will be entirely yours. Care must be taken, and control learned, when practising in the controlled arena, it is very easy for these techniques to break limbs without intention, when the opponent taps out release immediately. It is not good form to bend or squeeze a little more after the opponent has tapped, you do it to him and he'll probably do just the same to you. Where you release to the tap in a controlled fight you snap in a real fight (or you have the choice to snap), and where you gently bend the limb in the controlled arena you wrench at speed out side.

Note: There are several bars that can be employed from your back, and from a kneeling position, in order to keep the books in the series categorical. I have not entered them in this text, they will be covered in detail in Volumes 5 & 6.

Chapter One

From the Mount position

As I have stated in every book in this series, the mount position is probably the most potent pin of them all with many finishing possibilities, and easy access to the standing position should you require. Basically the pin is best employed as a podium from which to attack and turn the opponent for the devastating reverse mount strangle (see Vol 3 - Chokes and strangles). There are, however, one or two very fast arm bars that are very accessible from the mount and that can end an altercation in a split second - they need plenty of practice and a 'feel' (a 'feel' is an intangible thing that cannot really be taught, rather the practitioner has to earn it with hundreds of hours flight time) needs to be found to really make them work.

In the controlled arena, when the fights are all out with very few holds barred, 50% of my victories come via the arm bar (the other 50% Approx. come via the choke and strangle), ironically the opponent feeds the arm to you on the majority of occasions in his bid to attack you or to escape. The best techniques are the ones that the opponent gives you (inadvertently) and not those that you have to force. I generally precede my arm bars with a strike, this distracts the opponent giving me a blind second to take the bar.

The Grapevine

In all honesty I do not find this a very strong bar but it can work on some people so it is worth a mention, it is also a good way of tying an opponent's arm of so that you can hit him with your free hand, it's very hard for an opponent to defend his face with only one arm. The grapevine works really well whilst the opponent is compliant, ie in drilling work, but when

Arm Bars and Locks

compliancy is taken away most opponent's manage to struggle free after a few seconds, though that may be all you need to destroy an opponent from this position. Again we are not chasing this technique rather we are waiting for the opponent to offer it to us, this he will do in the form of grabbing or attempted striking. As his arm left (or right) grabs at your collar/shirt etc. wrap your left arm around it at the elbow, from your left to your right, so that his hand is palm up under your arm pit, grab your left and with your right hand and lean back and place pressure on his elbow joint.

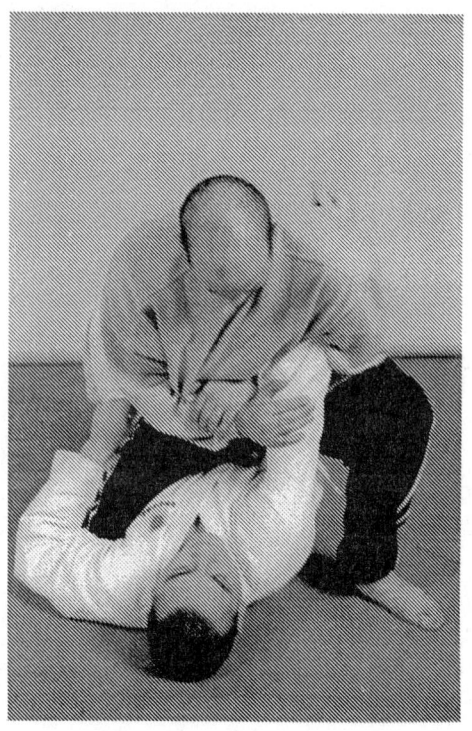

Ground Fighting: Volume Four

Shoulder lock

Grab the opponent's outstretched left arm with your right hand to pin in place, turn your body to your own right and sit through to your right with your left foot, simultaneously grip the opponent's arm with your left hand also. This will turn the opponent onto his side. From here sit slightly forward so that your weight is on his straightened arm, this will place pressure on his elbow joint, if your pull back hard on his arm it will break the elbow joint.

Arm Bars and Locks

Straight sitting arm bar

From the shoulder lock position you have the option to sit backwards so that the opponent's outstretched arm is between your legs and your feet are across his face, as per illustration. Pull down on his arm (it should be either palm up or little finger up for best effect) and push up against his elbow joint with your hips, to snap the joint yank down sharply with your hands and push sharply up with your hips.

Ground Fighting: Volume Four

Roll Forward

If you roll him a little more forward and sit your weight on his shoulder it will move the lock to a shoulder lock that, if forced will take the shoulder out of joint.

Reverse arm bar

If you roll completely forward so that you are on your belly, still gripping his straightened arm with both hands, you fall automatically into a reverse arm bar. For best effect hook your left foot in front of the opponent's face and pull back on his arm-you'll know when it is on, he'll shout the house down.

Ground Fighting: Volume Four

Standing arm bar

The opponent often tries to stand from this position, if the lock is on he will not be able to. If it is not completely on he will probably try, keep hold of his arm and keep your feet in the same position and wrench his arm back across your hip, against his elbow joint.

Straight sitting arm bar

From standing arm bar you can force the opponent over onto his back and into the straight sitting arm bar position, infact if you get the standing lock on this is probably the way he will want to go to try and escape the pain (or onto his belly where the reverse arm bar will automatically be on anyway). Push your left foot against his face so that his head is forced backwards, simultaneously pull back on the opponent's arm, this will unsettle his balance and force him to fall to his back. His outstretched arm will be between your legs and your feet are across his face, as per illustration. Pull down on his arm (it should be either palm up or little finger up for best effect) and push up against his elbow joint with your hips, to snap the joint yank down sharply with your hands and push sharply up with your hips.

Ground Fighting: Volume Four

Full Juji Gatame (Arm bar)

In the same fashion as the other locks first grip the opponent's left arm with your right hand, sit through with your left leg and fall to your back, still gripping his arm, but now with both hands, his hand should be palm up. His outstretched arm will be between your legs and your feet across his face, as per illustration. Pull down on his arm (it should be either palm up or little finger up for best effect) and push up against his elbow joint with your hips, to snap the joint yank down sharply with your hands and push sharply up with your hips.

Ground Fighting: Volume Four

Roll through

If the opponent rolls as you go for the lock and resists so that you cannot complete the bar don't fight too hard for it just go with the flow and roll with him so that you are on your belly and his arm is in the reverse arm bar position. Pull the arm back and push your hips forward against his elbow.

Arm Bars and Locks

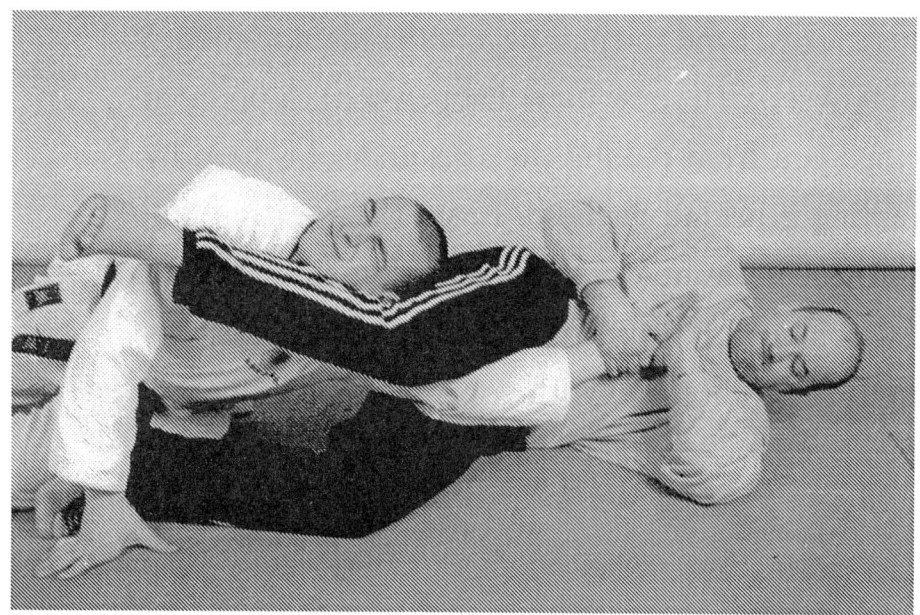

The same as the other techniques, if the opponent stands you can utilise the standing bar by pulling his arm across your hip or force him to his back to the sitting arm bar by pushing your foot across his face and wrenching on his arm.

Triangular arm twist

As detailed in Vol 3 chokes and strangles and in Vol One the pins, an excellent method of turning the opponent onto his belly is by knocking his arm across his body and lying on it, trapping it across his neck with your chest, then feeding your left arm under his head, from your left to your right, and grabbing his trapped hand and pulling it under his head to turn him over, what some times happens is the opponent stops you from pulling the arm under his head by pulling it behind his head. From this position pull the hand in an anti-clock wise direction, towards your own chest with your left hand and pushing his elbow in the same direction with your right hand, this will make the bar.

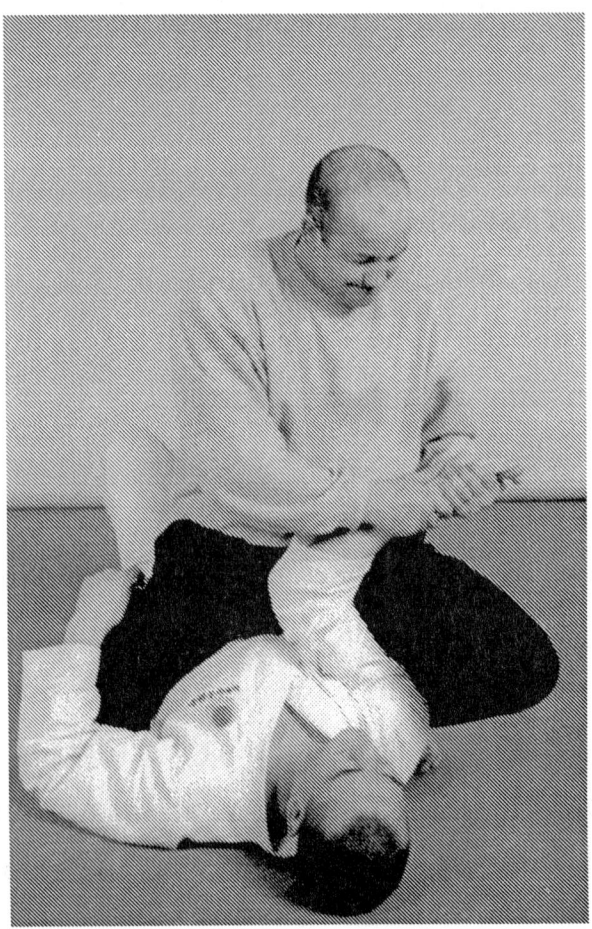

Arm Bars and Locks

Sometimes it is possible to take finger bars and wrist locks from this position, as it is from most positions. Basically whenever the opponent's hands are in range you can attack the fingers and wrists. I will cover these in a later chapter. These are, really, rainy day techniques that I do not look for but neither do I pass up if they are offered, they are especially good when trying to break an opponent's grip.

Chapter Two

From the Scarf Hold

Some of the bars and locks in this chapter were touched on/covered in the first volume on Pins but because I cannot presume that the reader has read the first volume I shall repeat them here also. If you did read the first volume please accept my apologies for repeating (though of course they do stand repeating).

If the opponent's right arm gets free from under your left arm you can use one of several bars and locks.

1) Bar it over your right leg. Push his right arm, at the elbow and palm up, across your right thigh.

Arm Bars and Locks

2) Bar it over your left leg. If his arm will not straighten switch legs to create a higher fulcrum by bringing your left leg through and pushing your right leg back and bar it over your left leg.

3) Back to right leg bar. If the opponent is still struggling then quickly switch back your legs and drive his arm, at the elbow joint, into/over the lower fulcrum of your right leg.

Arm Bars and Locks

4) Left leg tie off. Tie his arm off under your reverse/left leg, to bar the turn your hips up to the ceiling and push.

5) Right leg tie off. In his bid to stop you tying off his arm under your left leg the opponent may direct his energy towards your right leg, if so quickly tie it off under your right leg, to make the lock more secure and painful wrap your left leg around the foot of your left leg and pull back with your left leg.

Juji Gatame (arm bar)

Release your right arm from under the opponent head and place it straight out in front of you. Step across the opponent's body and place your left foot at the left (far) side of his head. At the same time bring your right leg to the right side of his body and bring your right arm back to grip his right arm, ensure that at all times you keep control of his right arm with your left and right. Sit back and trap the opponent's head with your left leg, simultaneously

Arm Bars and Locks

wedge your right foot underneath his body at his right hand side. His arm is between your legs, pull down on his arm and push up with your hips to complete the bar. This is a very difficult position to take the arm bar from, much practice will be needed to make it smooth, once you have the technique however you will catch many opponents.

Jack-knife escape into arm bar

Again the jack-knife escape is detailed heavily in Volume 2 of this series, Escapes, and should be referred to for finer detail. Separate your chest from your opponent's back whilst simultaneously poking him in the throat with your left hand to force him backwards. As he falls onto his back he will probably keep hold of the head lock he has on you (if he has any sense at all). At this point you will be kneeling at the opponent's side, place your right foot over his head and base it on the floor by the left side of his face. Poke your finger in his eye to get him to release

Arm Bars and Locks

his grip from your head, as he does his arm will straighten. Lie onto your back and trap the opponent's head with your left leg, simultaneously wedge your right foot underneath his body at his right hand side. His arm is between your legs, pull down on his arm and push up with your hips to complete the bar.

Ground Fighting: Volume Four

Arm Bars and Locks

Shoulder Lock

It is also an option from the kneeling position to take a forward shoulder lock. Force the opponent's arm straight, same as before by punching him in the face or poking his eyes/face/throat with your fingers until he releases. When he does his arm will straighten, step over his body with your right leg and kneel across his face with your left leg, sit forward onto the arm to make the hold.

Reverse Arm Bar

If the opponent forces you forward onto your belly, or you wish to go forward onto your belly to take the reverse arm bar, fall forward being sure to keep control of the opponent's arm and force your left foot in front of his face, pull his arm into your body to make the lock. If he tries to stand up you can, again, follow and execute a standing arm bar or force the opponent over onto his back for the sitting arm bar. One hold very much runs into another-if you go with the flow the opponent will not escape the lock (unless his arm breaks of course).

Chapter Three

From the upper 4 1/4 pin.

This is not my favourite place to take arm bars from, I use the pin more as a travellers rest hold. Having watched a lot of the American shoot fighting (this is very much all out fighting where compliancy is rarer than a tax rebate) and they very much favour taking the arm bars from the upper 4 1/4 position, especially the Juji Gatame arm bar, and they are expert at it too. Other excellent ground fighters like the brilliant Neil Adams also take the arms bars, especially Juji Gatame from just about every position you could think off. But these fighters are innovators who constantly break tradition to find new concepts and better techniques. There is nothing stopping you (who ever you are) doing exactly the same.

Arm Bars and Locks

Tradition is great for acquiring a firm foundation, but sometimes you have to break down the walls of conventional acceptance if you want to be different, to be better. When I first left the KUGB, with whom I had been, on and off, for twenty years, lots of people slagged me off and said that I had sold out (though funnily enough I do not remember any of them actually saying that to my face) and that I had lost my way etc etc etc. But I had the confidence in myself and in what I was doing to cope with that criticism because I knew that they were wrong and that it was spread by jealous people that wanted to do what I had done but didn't have the moral fibre (most of them couldn't even spell it).

Now I never left the KUGB because it was a bad association, infact I think that it is one of the finest associations in the world run by some of the finest martial artists in the world (just put my cheque in the post lads), I never left because I was a disgruntled member, on the contrary, the standards were high and every one was happy with it. I left because I had found my own direction, my own way and so I followed my heart and did my own thing, as I am still doing today. But if I had stayed where I was because of the locals that thought I was selling out I'd have still been an average Karate man in a very big association - change is sense not sacrilege. So break a few rules, search for new techniques, explore, expand and get exited about how much there is out there to learn-my only worry now is whether my life time is going to be long enough to fit in all the things that I haven't quite learned yet. I digress-the upper 4 1/4.

Juji Gatame

Rather than take the arm bar from the conventional upper 4 1/4, this would make for slow movement, come to a crouching position over the opponent, as illus. He will feed one arm or the other to try and escape (if he feeds both you have a choice as to whether to go to the left or the right). If he feeds his right arm the take hold of it with your left hand and quickly turn to your own right and place your left leg over his face and plant it net to the right side of his head.

Arm Bars and Locks

Lie onto your back and trap the opponent's head with your left leg, simultaneously wedge your right foot underneath his body at his left hand side. His arm will be between your legs, pull down on his arm and push up with your hips to complete the bar. If he rolls forward to block the bar roll with him onto your own belly and execute the reverse arm bar, if he stands up take the standing arm bar or force him over on to his back and into the conventional juji Gatame. If the opponent feed the opposite arm, when you are in the upper 4 1/4 go the opposite way and reverse the latter instructions.

Ground Fighting: Volume Four

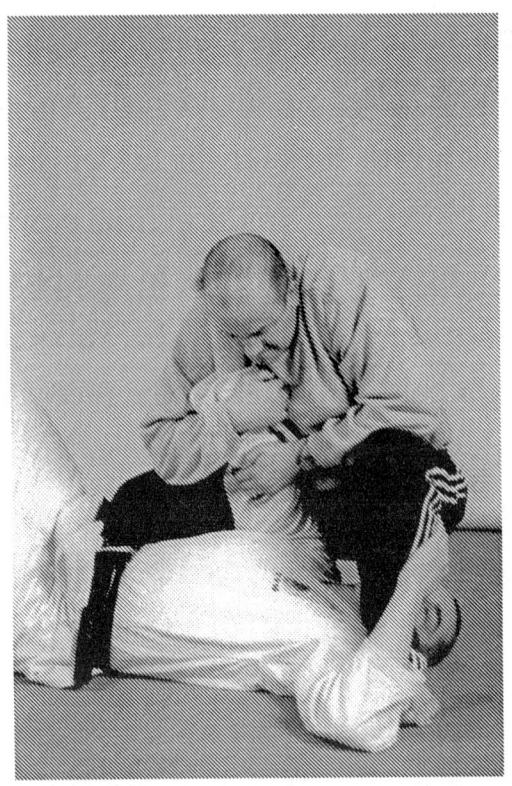

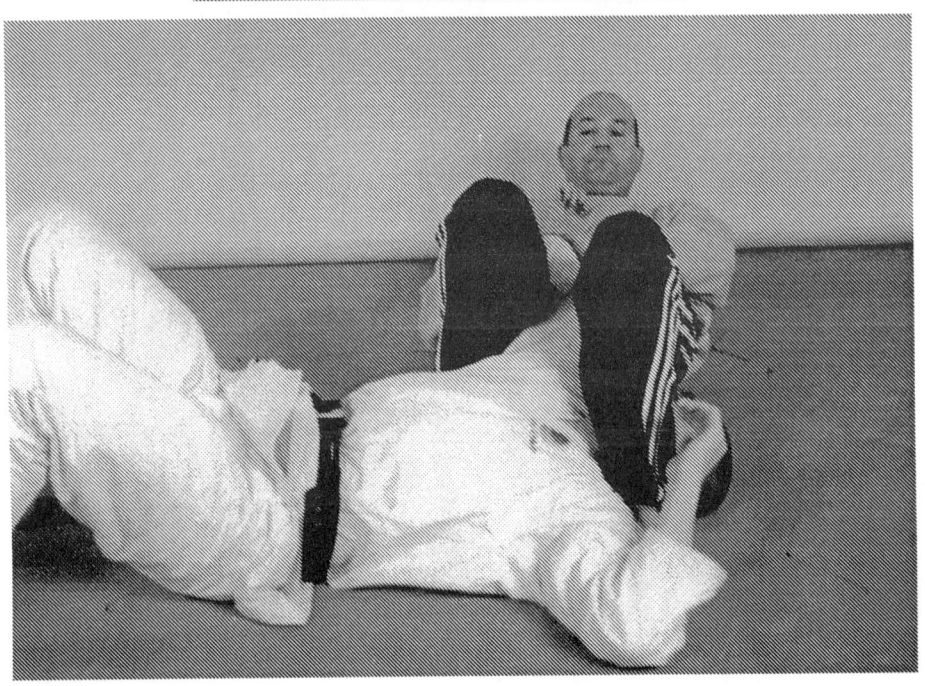

Turn and Bar

If, when holding the opponent in the upper 4 1/4, he turns onto his belly loop your right arm (or left) under his left arm pit and pull him over on to his back, place your left leg over his face and plant it next to the right side of his head. Lie onto your back and trap the opponent's head with your left leg, simultaneously wedge your right foot underneath his body at his left hand side. His arm will be between your legs, pull down on his arm and push up with your hips to complete the bar. The usual extras, reverse arm bar, standing arm bar and force down into sitting arm bar also apply if the opponent feeds you the necessary energy.

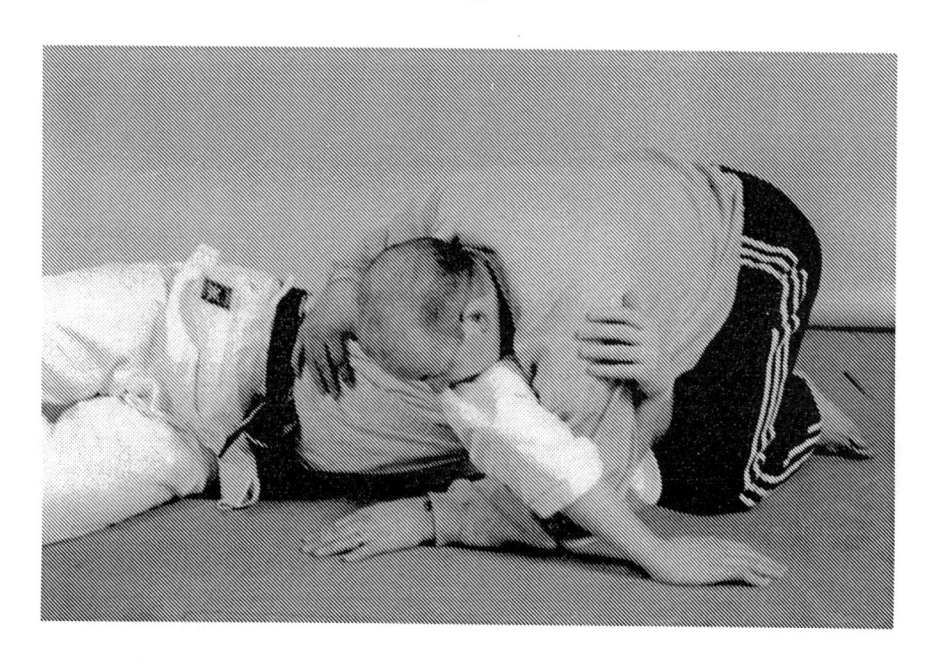

Ground Fighting: Volume Four

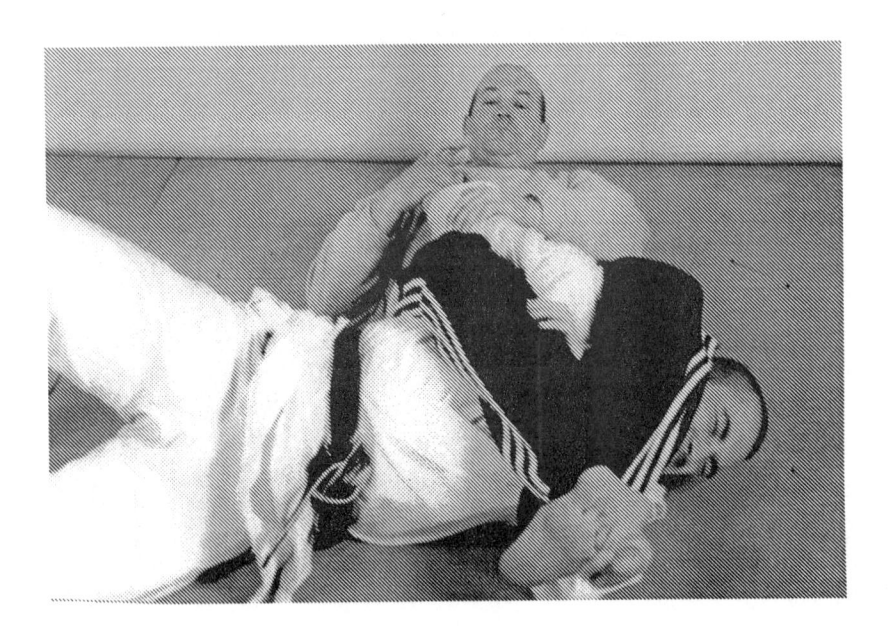

Arm Bars and Locks

Arm pit shoulder bar

Again, if the opponent rolls onto his belly in a bid to escape hook his left arm under the elbow with your right arm and sit though into the reverse scarf hold position, only with your arms on the out side as opposed to around his neck, and sit all your weight so that your left arm pit is across his left shoulder. As you sit your weight on his shoulder pull up with both hands on his outstretched arm, keep his palm downward. This can be taken to either side of the opponent.

Ground Fighting: Volume Four

Reverse mount Juji Gatame

If the opponent rolls onto his belly quickly spin around on his back and take the reverse mount position, allow him a little room so that he is tempted to try and turn back onto his back. As he does, take his left arm (right arm if he tries to turn from the opposite side) and pull him to his back, as he turns place your left leg over his face and plant it next to the right side of his head.

Arm Bars and Locks

Lie onto your back and trap the opponent's head with your left leg, simultaneously wedge your right foot underneath his body at his left hand side. His arm will be between your legs, pull down on his arm and push up with your hips to complete the bar. The usual extras, reverse arm bar, standing arm bar and force down into sitting arm bar also apply if the opponent feeds you the necessary energy. Alternatively if the opponent does not take the bait and turn but tries to push into a kind of press up position to escape then, again, take his left arm (or right arm) and pull him to his back, as he turns place your left leg over his face and plant it next to the right side of his head.

Ground Fighting: Volume Four

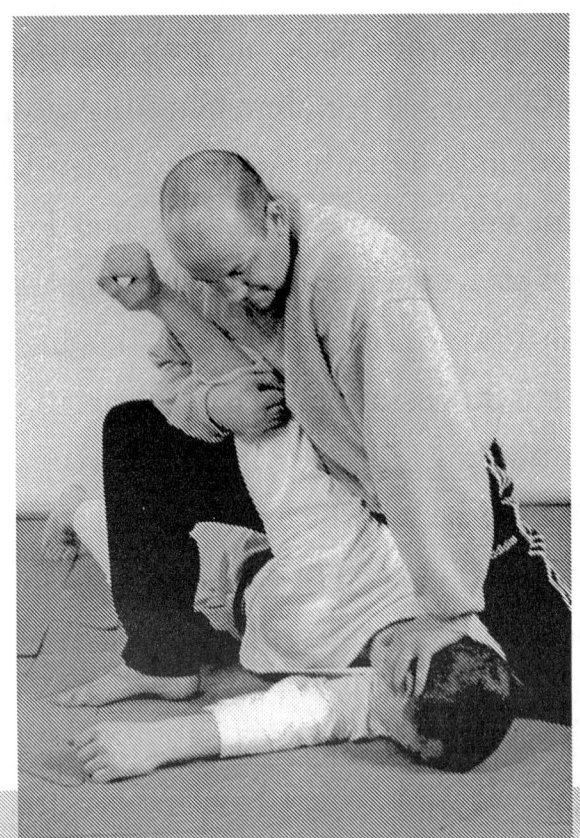

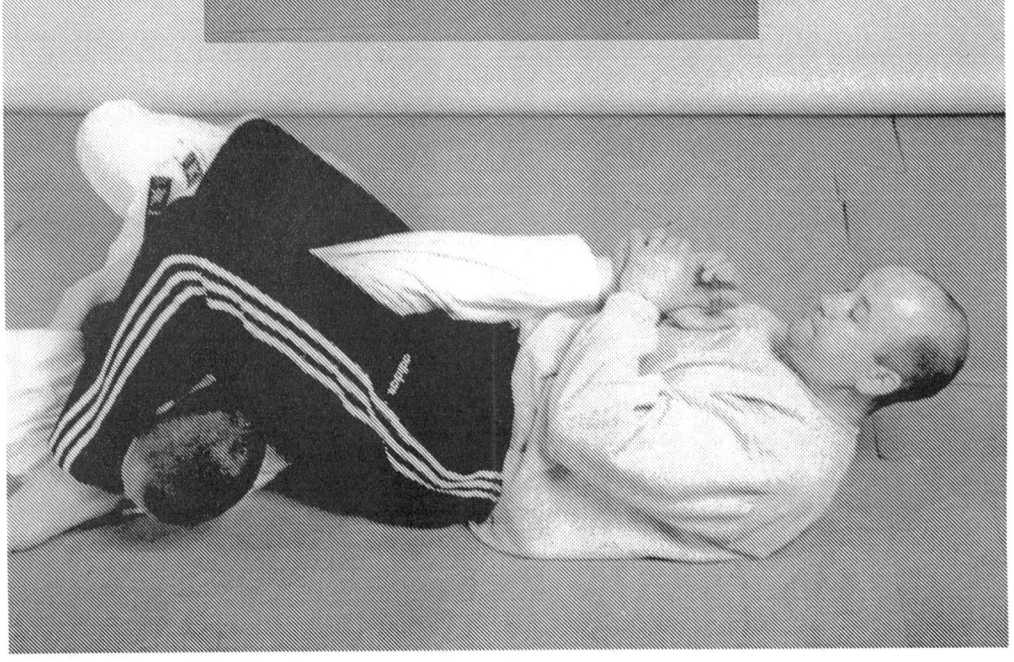

58

Arm Bars and Locks

Front mount arm bar

Spin from the upper 4 1/4 position into the mount position. Whichever arm the opponent feeds you take and sit through, as pre described into the conventional juji Gatame from the mount position. If you spin to the mount from the left, try and take the opponent's left arm (or if spinning from the right his right arm) so that you can use the momentum of the spin to take the bar fast and smooth.

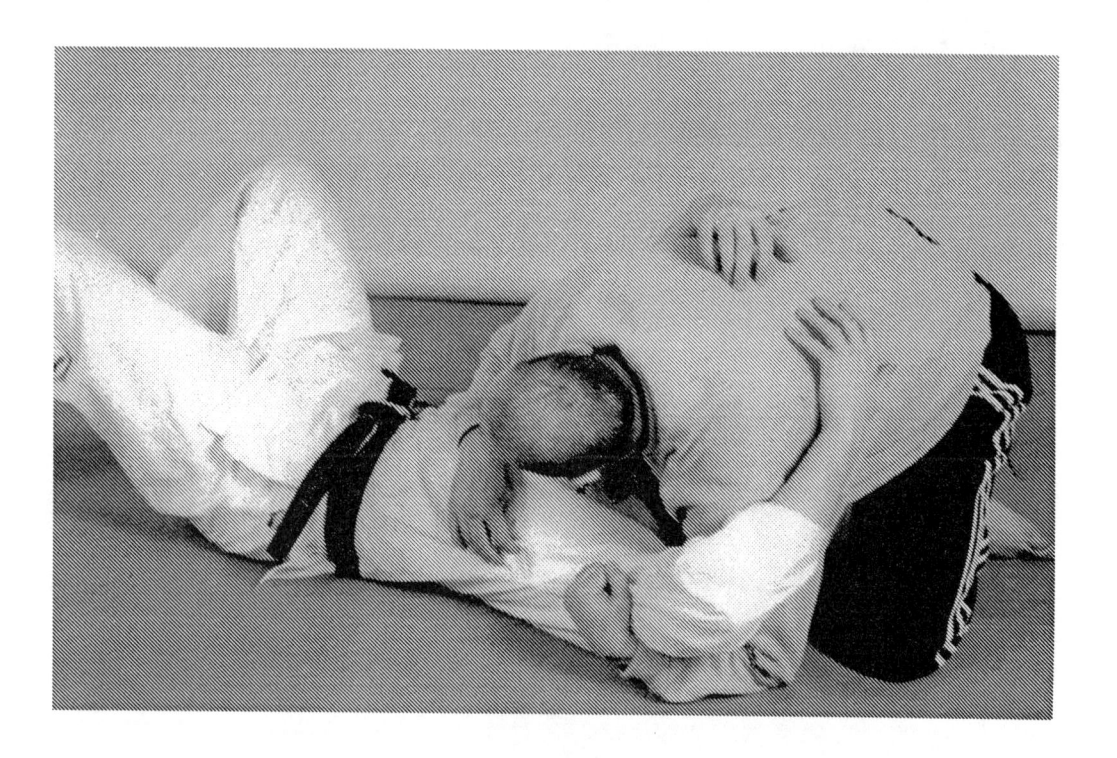

Ground Fighting: Volume Four

60

Arm Bars and Locks

Chapter Four

From the Side 4 1/4 Hold Down.

This is another travellers rest hold that is better suited as a resting place, it is very easy to defend and excellent for getting to the more potent mount position or even the scarf hold, however there are some bars that can be taken from this position (also chokes and strangles-covered in Vol 3 of this series).

Juji Gatame (arm bar); First come to the shortened version of the side 4 1/4 (knees up), catch hold of his right arm with your right hand and place your left leg over his face, making sure that your leg goes underneath his right arm, and plant it next to the right side of his head. Keep control of his arm at all times. Lie onto your back and trap the opponent's head with your left leg, simultaneously wedge your right foot underneath his body at his left hand side. His arm will be between your legs, pull down on his arm and push up with your hips to complete the bar. The usual extras, reverse arm bar, standing arm bar and force down into sitting arm bar also apply if the opponent feeds you the necessary energy. As with taking the bar from the scarf hold taking it from the side 4 1/4 is an advanced technique that will need many hours of flight time to perfect.

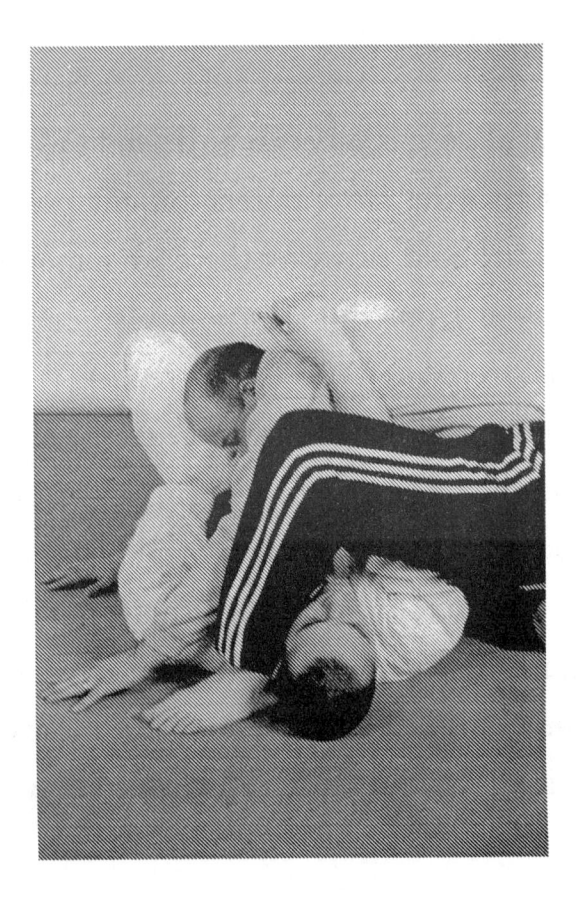

Figure 4 arm lock

Reach over and grab the opponent's left wrist (his palm facing up) with your left hand, feed your right arm underneath his left arm and grip your own left wrist, as per illus. Force his wrist down to the floor with your left hand and force his elbow off the floor and backwards with your right arm to make the lock. This is more of a way of locking the opponent's arm than anything else but it can also act as a good bar if you get the grip.

It is worth remembering however that, if the bar is not on and it is not causing the opponent discomfort, then all you are doing is pinning him and in doing so you are also tying up your own arm when they could be doing something more potent.

Figure 4 to straight arm bar

In his struggle to escape the figure 4 the opponent's energy often forces his arm straight. If this is the case let his arm straighten and, using the grip that you already hold, bar his arm at his elbow joint by pushing down on his wrist with your left hand and forcing up against his elbow joint with your right arm.

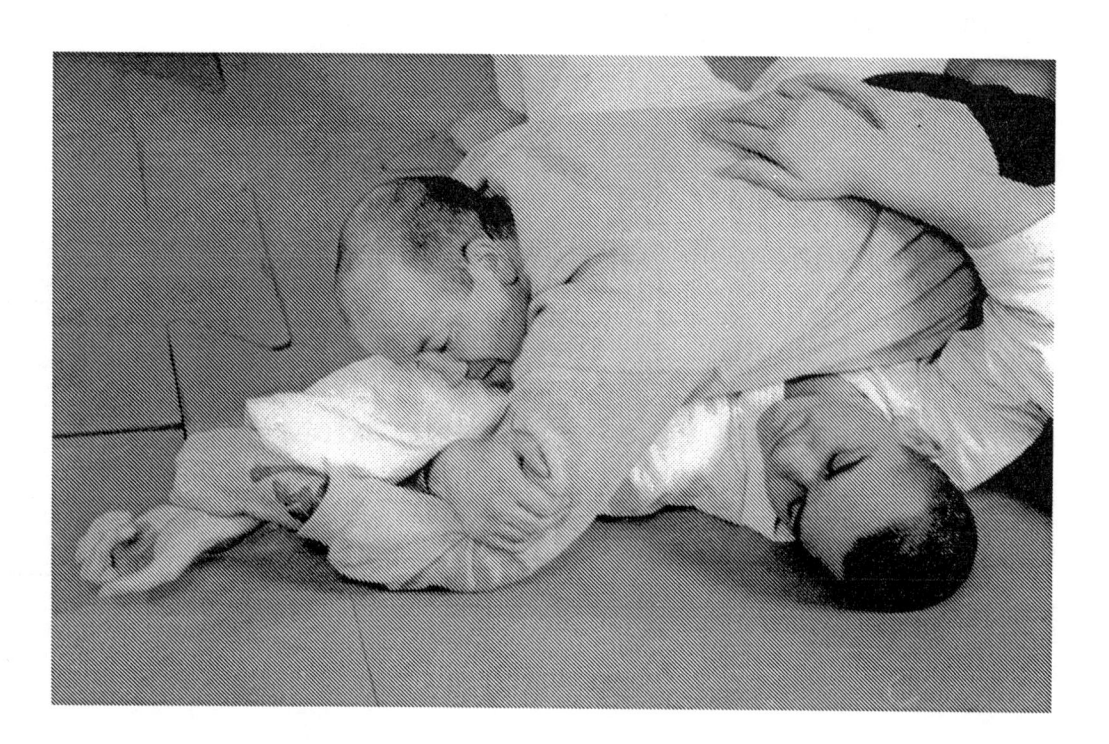

Side 4 1/4 to mount arm bar

Sit through into the mount position, as you do so grab the opponent's left arm and sit straight through to the otherside by placing your right leg over his face and plant it next to the right side of his head. Keep control of his arm at all times. Lie onto your back and trap the opponent's head with your left leg, simultaneously wedge your right foot underneath his body at his left hand side. His arm will be between your legs, pull down on his arm and push up with your hips to complete the bar. If, when you sit into the mount position, the opponent feeds you his opposite arm then take the bar the opposite way, to your own left instead of your own right, and simply reverse the latter instructions. The usual extras, reverse arm bar, standing arm bar and force down into sitting arm bar also apply if the opponent feeds you the necessary energy.

Arm Bars and Locks

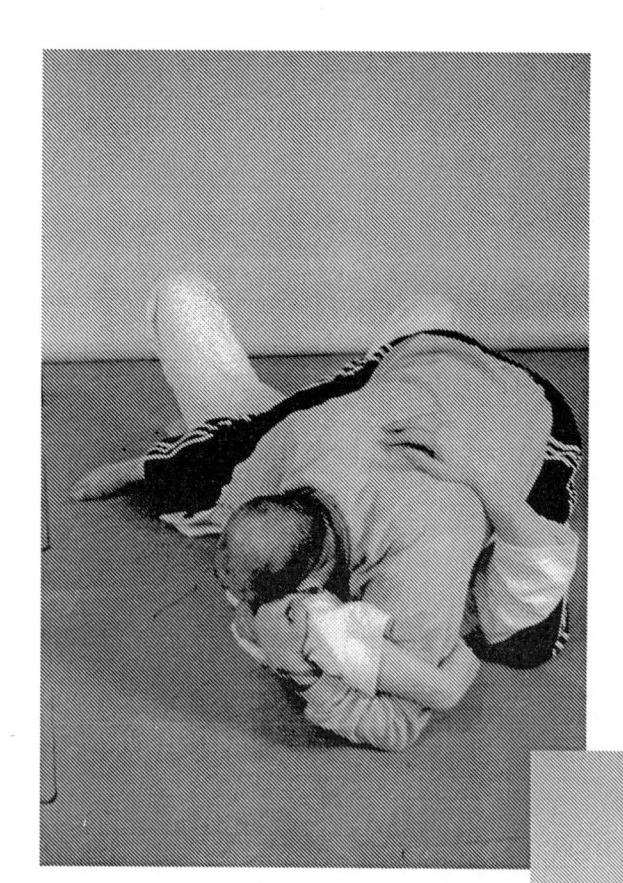

67

Reverse Mount arm bar

If, when holding the opponent in the side 4 1/4, he turns onto his belly (this is very usual with many inexperienced ground fighters. They see this as a good means of escape where as in actuality it is the worst thing they can do if they are fighting someone with ground fighting knowledge) sit onto his back in the reverse mount and loop your right arm (or left) under his left arm pit and pull him over on to his back, as he does so place your left leg over his face and plant it next to the right side of his head.

Arm Bars and Locks

Lie onto your back and trap the opponent's head with your left leg, simultaneously wedge your right foot underneath his body at his left hand side. His arm will be between your legs, pull down on his arm and push up with your hips to complete the bar. The usual extras, reverse arm bar, standing arm bar and force down into sitting arm bar also apply if the opponent feeds you the necessary energy.

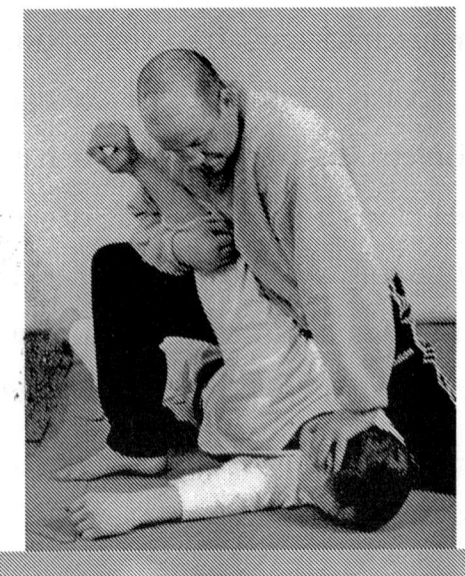

Arm pit shoulder bar

Again, if the opponent rolls onto his belly in a bid to escape, hook his left arm under his elbow with your right arm and sit through into the reverse scarf hold position, only with your arms on the out side as opposed to around his neck. Sit all your weight so that your left arm pit is across his left shoulder. As

Arm Bars and Locks

you sit your weight on his shoulder pull up with both hands on his outstretched arm, keep his palm downward.

71

Chapter Five

Leg Bars from the opponent's scissor guard

A very familiar place to end up in is the opponent's scissor guard. A good ground fighter can hold an opponent here for a very long time, appropriately the scissor guard is also the innate safety mechanism used by fighters in a street situation that find themselves on their backs. When the opponent locks his legs around your waist it can be a very difficult place from which to escape. An experienced ground fighter will use a scissor guard to rest and also to force an impatient fighter to make a mistake. When he does he'll take advantage and finish the fight from his back with arm bars, chokes, turns etc (to be detailed in Vol 5 of this series Fighting from your back).

There are one or two reliable escapes from the opponent's scissor guard that will enable you to attack his legs with locks and bars, or climb through into the mount position and finish from there. With practice it is possible to break an opponent's limbs with the following locks but, from my experience, it takes a lot of flight time to get it right so practice is the imperative once again.

Inner Thigh attack

Bring your right (or left) arm forward towards the opponent's head and then sharply back so that your elbow strikes sharply into the nerve point on the opponent's inner thigh, this will break his guard. Alternatively you can use your thumb to press the nerve and get the same effect. The nerve is only small and is situated right in the centre of the inner thigh, so it may take a few strikes to get it on the button, keep striking or poking until his guard is broken.

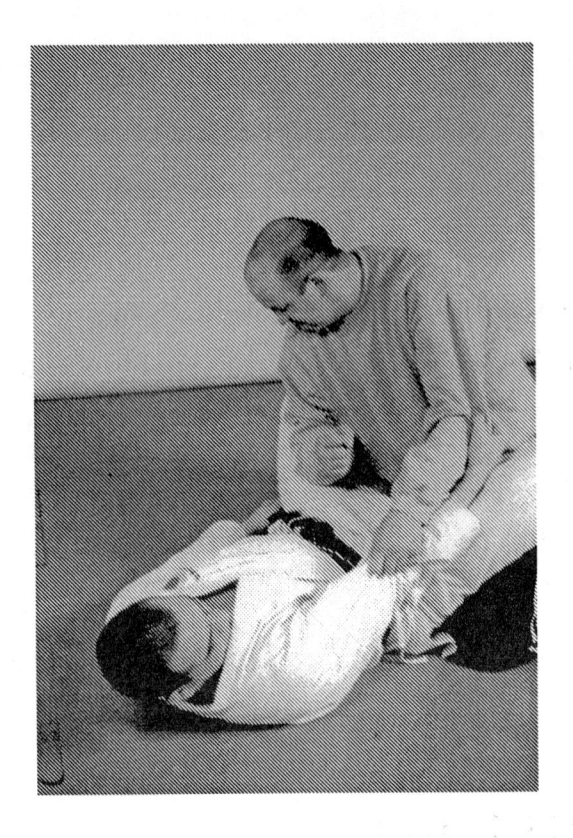

Groin attack

Reach down to the opponent's groin and poke your thumb into his ingual canal. This is situated about an inch to the left and an inch higher than the pubic bone, both sides (right at the top of the thigh by the groin area), again this is usually good for breaking down the guard. If you cannot find it then grab the opponent by the testicles and squeeze and pull and rip, this will move his guard down.

Arm Bars and Locks

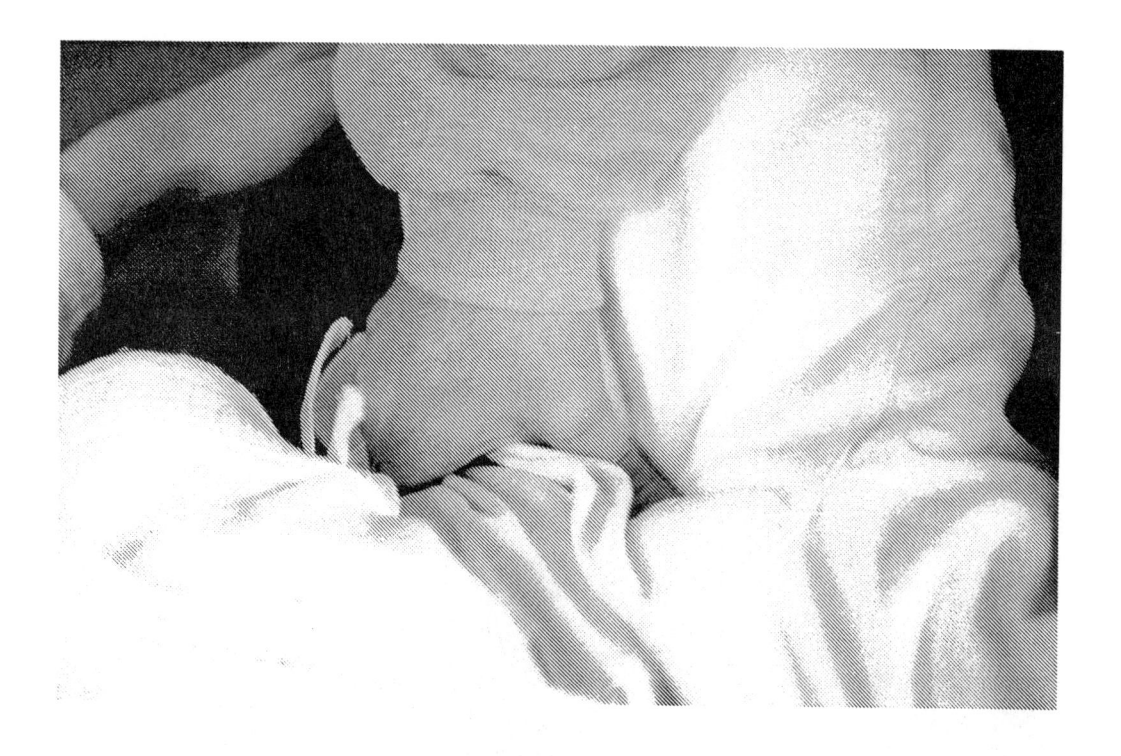

Leg sweep

Force your right arm (or left) between the opponent's legs (at your right hand side) and sweep the opponent's legs over and past your head the move down into the side 4 1/4 pin. This is not an easy technique, but it is one that does work on some opponent's, but it can be used in conjunction with the others, ie. strike the opponent's inner thigh and as his guard breaks push your arm through and sweep his legs around to the side.

Ground Fighting: Volume Four

Arm Bars and Locks

Back slam

If you are struggling to break the opponent's guard you can use the back slam, though this does take an awful lot of back and leg strength. Reach through and grab the opponent's lapels (or any appendage) with both hands, stand up lifting the opponent and slam his back into the floor. (this would work particularly well in the street scenario if you could drop the opponent onto an uneven surface like a curb etc). This will knock the wind out of him and force his guard to break, often the opponent will break his guard as soon as you lift him off the ground.

Ground Fighting: Volume Four

Boston Crab

Although you will have seen this technique probably a thousand times on the show wrestling on TV and thought nothing of it because show wrestling is often seen as unrealistic this technique is actually a very dangerous and effective move. It was the favourite finishing technique of the legendary English wrestler Bert Asarati, who had over seven thousand bouts and held the British Title for 25 years (I will soon be releasing a book on Mr Asarati called 'One Man One Riot').

Grab the opponent's legs, from the outside in and round the back of his knees, with both arms and stand up, force the opponent, to your right (or left), onto his belly and step over his back with your left leg, sit onto his back and pull back hard on his legs. Be very careful in training otherwise there will be discs popping out all over the place. Never fall back onto the opponent's back otherwise you might easily break it. If you let go of the legs you are already in a vertical position whilst the opponent is still on the floor.

Arm Bars and Locks

Ground Fighting: Volume Four

Half Boston crab

The same applies with the Half Boston Crab, only now you are using only one of the opponent legs (either one will do). Grab the opponent's right leg with your left arm underneath the knee so that his foot is under your arm pit, couple your left and right hand to secure the hold. Force him onto his belly, step over his back with your left leg, sit onto his back and pull back hard on his leg. Again be very careful in training other wise there will be discs popping out all over the place, never fall back onto the opponent's back otherwise you might easily break it. If you let go of the legs you are already in a vertical position whilst the opponent is still on the floor.

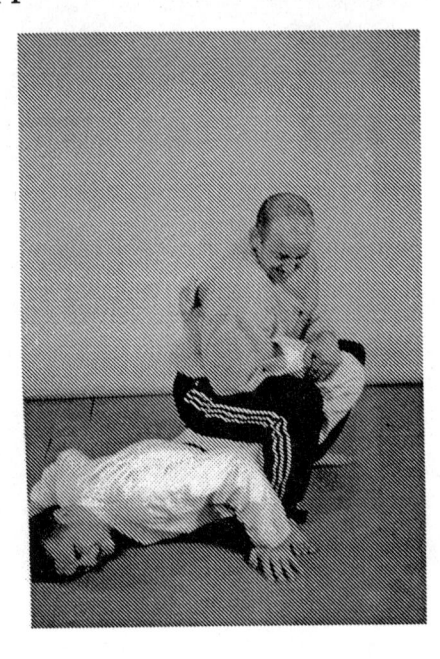

Standing ankle bar

Grab the opponent's right leg with your left arm so that the bone of the wrist is across the ankle bone (or the Achilles tendon or even the calf muscle), couple your left and your right hand to make the hold stronger. The opponent's foot should be under your arm pit. Lean back and force the wrist of your left arm hard against the opponent's ankle. If the opponent struggles from her you have the option to turn him into the Half Boston Crab.

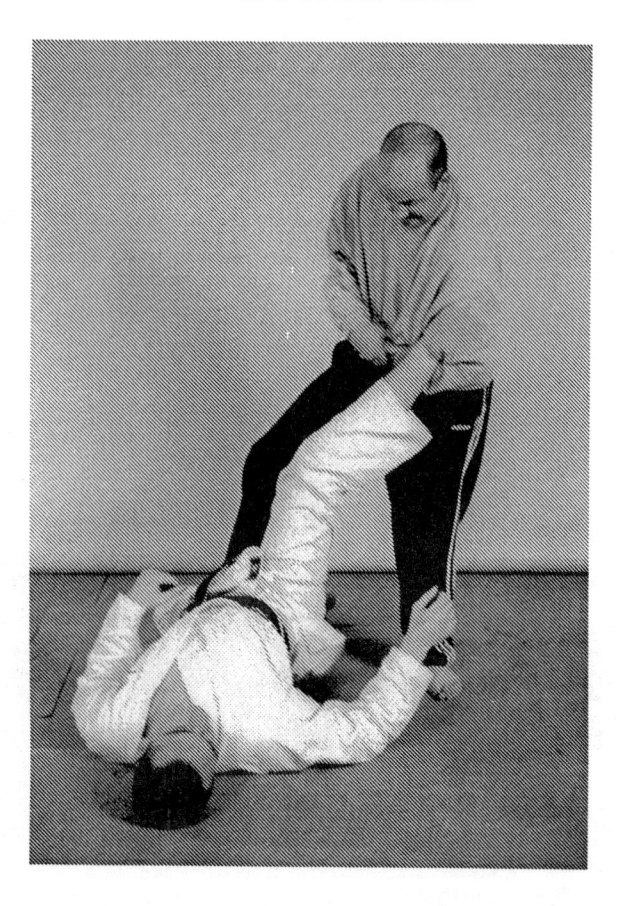

Sitting ankle bar

Or alternatively you can keep the same hold and sit down, wrenching at the ankle as you do so. On the floor wrap your right leg over the opponent's left and link it with your left leg. This will stop the opponent grabbing your leg and putting on the same hold. If he tries to sit up to escape the hold kick him in the chest or face with your right foot. Lean back and force the wrist of your left arm hard against the opponent's ankle.

Arm Bars and Locks

Crutch stretch and knee bar

Sweep your right hand under the opponent's left leg and stand up, step over his belly with your right leg in an anti-clockwise direction so that your back is now facing the opponent, keep hold of the leg, as per illus. Grip the opponent's leg with both hands at his foot and calf and sit back across the left side of the opponent's body and bring the leg with you. Use your groin as a fulcrum and bend his leg, at the knee, over it. At the same time put your right foot into his groin, at the very top of his right leg, and push.

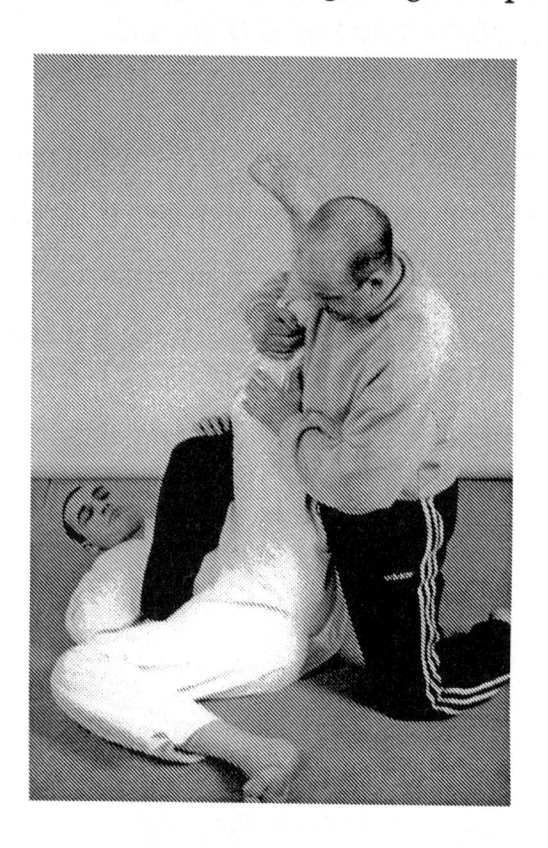

Ground Fighting: Volume Four

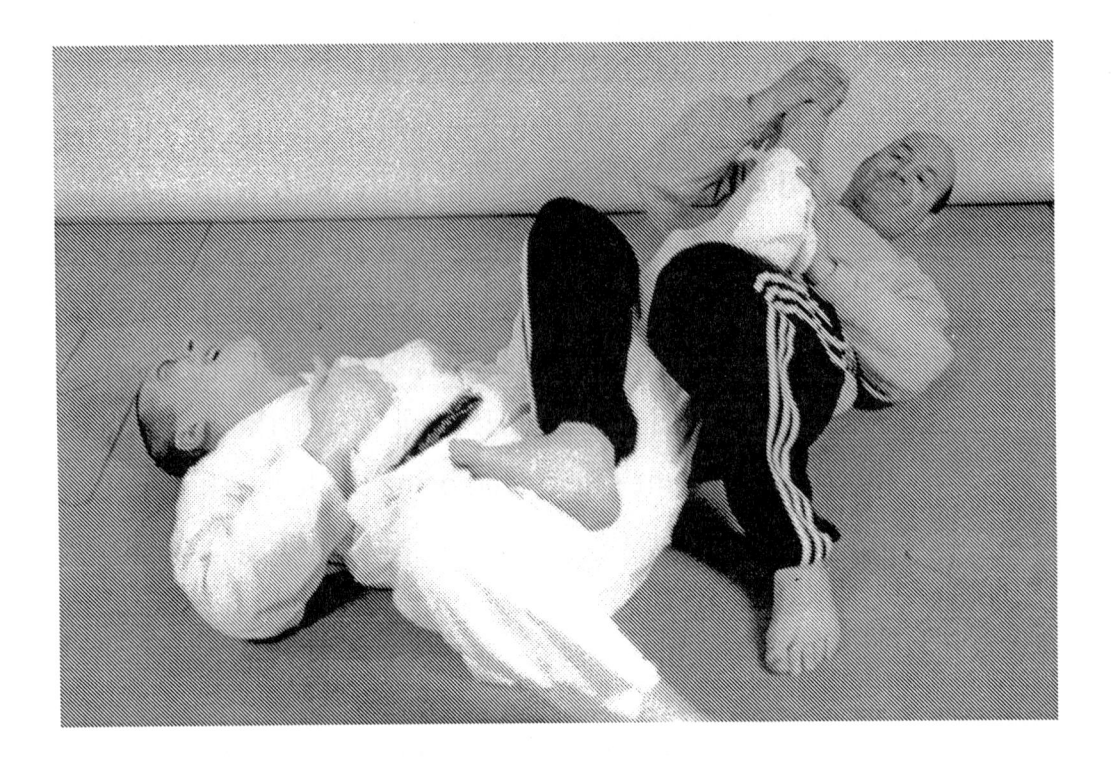

In honesty I do not really favour the leg bars, though I have seen some spectacular finishes with them, especially by the brilliant Ken Shamrock from the USA who seems to specialise in leg bar finishes.

Chapter Six

Finishing from Juji Gatame

In the sport of Judo where atemi is not allowed the art of finishing Juji Gatame has become quite a complex matter (that is, when you take the arm bar and the opponent interlinks his hands to block the bar).

In the world of real where atemi is the order of the day this is not such a complex matter, you simply give the opponent pain in another area so that he is forced, often subconsciously, to release his grip to defend that area. If I push my thumb in the opponent's eye he is going to have to release his grip on his own hand to stop me, in doing so he allows me the bar. Here are a few ideas to work on. If you want more detail on releases I highly recommend Neil Adams' book Arm locks, published by Ippon Books.

There are different schools of thought on technique and how to develop it. I try to develop it as close to the way, and the place, that I intend to use it as possible. Everything I train is either for my main artillery techniques in a real street defence situation or my support system for the same arena. If I train too much away from the realities of this I am, in a way, ill preparing myself for it. By disallowing strikes and bites in the controlled arena I am stripping the reality away from my artillery so that, when I do end up in a real encounter and an opponent gouges or bites me I may be beaten because in not training for those possibilities (or probabilities more like) I have not learned to defend against them.

As I said before, you get what you train for, muscle memory will print out what is on the memory banks and if you have to start thinking too much in a real encounter that thought, that indecision could cost you the fight. Because those in the sport side of fighting are not allowed to use the illegal techniques, as they are known, they have to devise techniques that are legal but that hold not real relevance in a real combat scenario. If my opponent grips his own hand to block a bar then I'll punch him in the head or poke him in the eye until he lets go-end of story.

The other side of the coin of course is that, in not allowing illegal techniques, one is forced to perfect the technique in hand and really fine tune it so that, perhaps, you can make the techniques work without it-this is a good thing and for this reason some of my training is devoted to restricted fighting to force and develop the use clean technique. But never forgetting that I am not training it for sport rather I am training it for the savage opponent on the street.

Wrist flex

This is a finishing technique on its own. Grab the opponent's hand, whichever one is uppermost and bend it forward at the wrist, when the pain hits, the opponent will release his grip and allow you to take the juji Gatame.

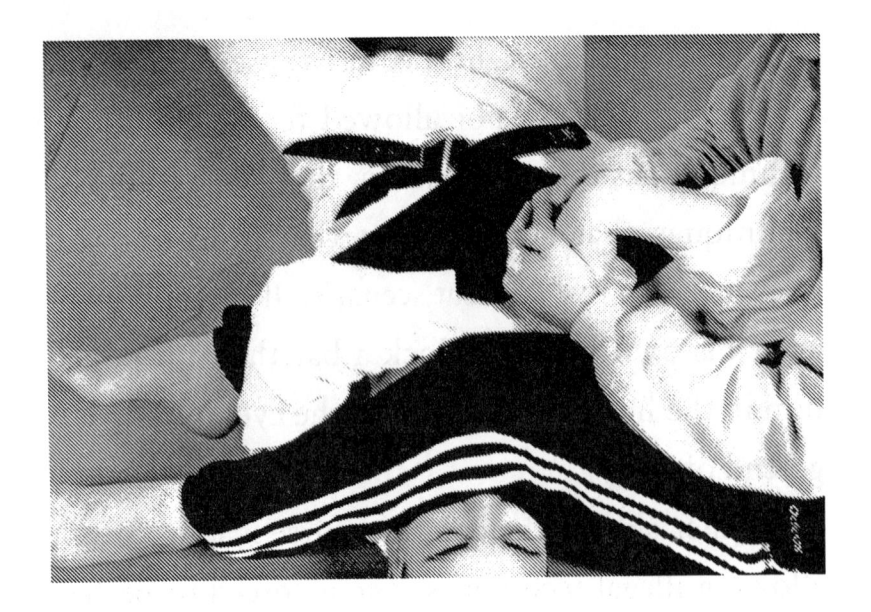

Finger bend

Grab the opponent's fingers, or thumb on the nearest hand and bend back hard, when the pain hits, the opponent will release his grip and allow you to take the juji Gatame.

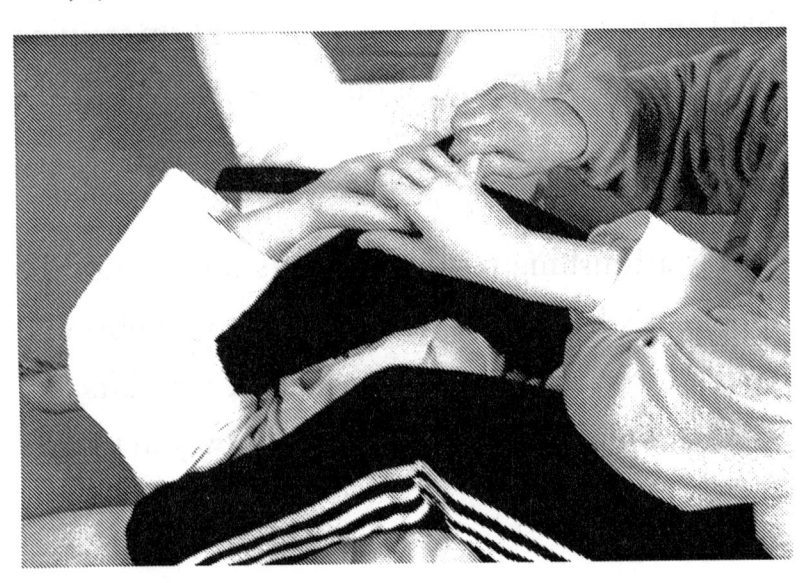

Arm Bars and Locks

Finger strike

Wrap the opponent's fingers with your right middle knuckles, when the pain hits, the opponent will release his grip and allow you to take the juji Gatame.

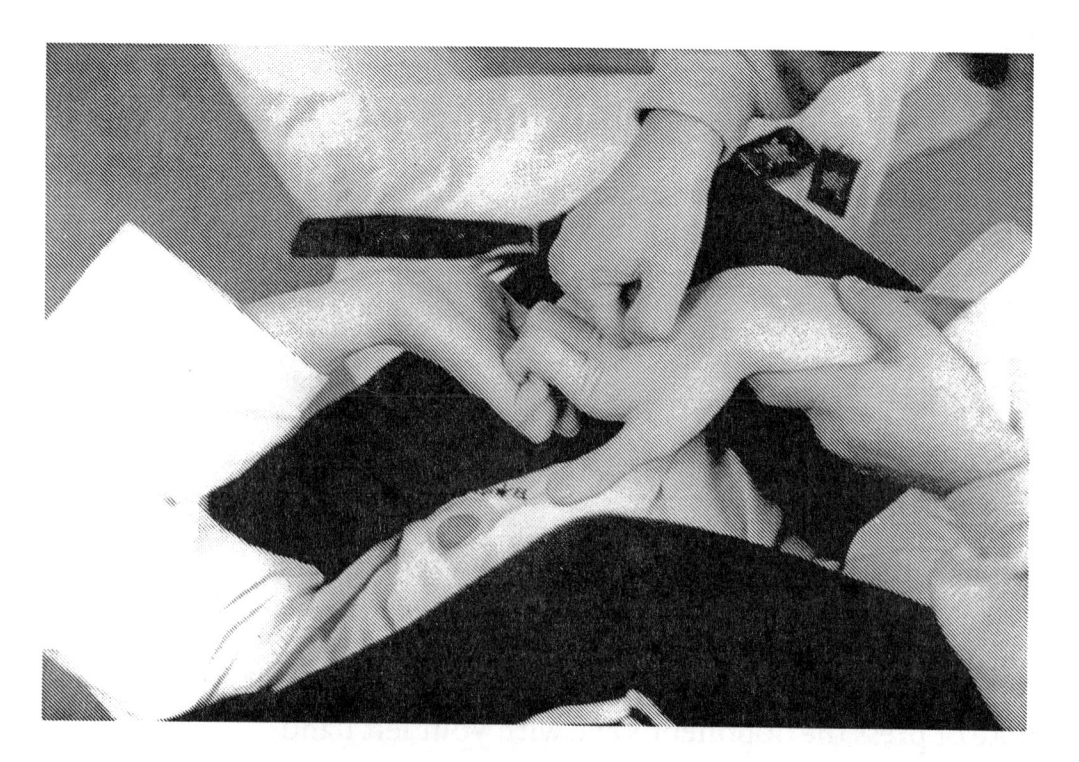

Kick and release

Lift up your right leg and axe kick the opponent in the ribs and groin until he releases his grip, when the pain hits, the opponent will release his grip and allow you to take the juji Gatame.

Kick biceps

Place your foot onto the opponent's biceps, the arm furthest away from you and kick or push with your leg to break his grip, when the opponent releases his grip take the juji Gatame.

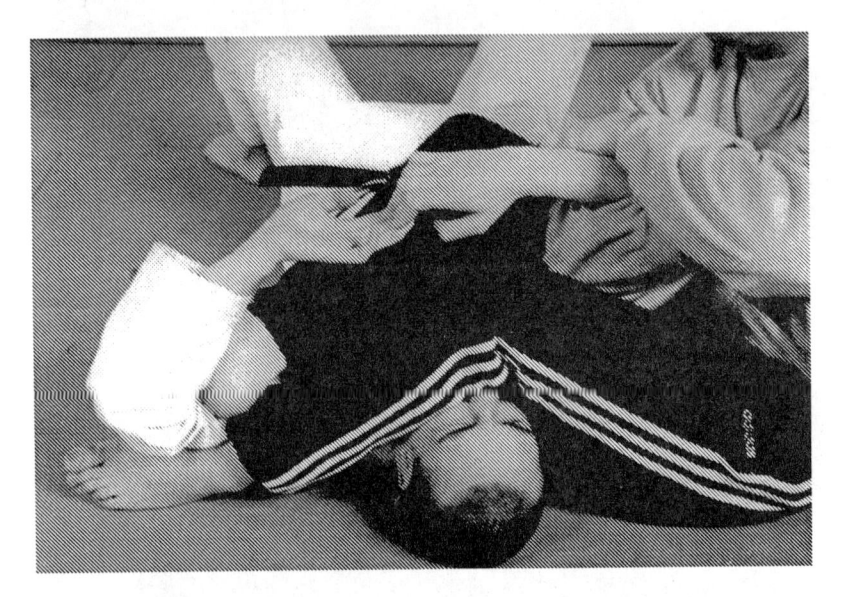

Eye poke

Poke or press the opponent's eye with your left hand, when the pain hits, the opponent will release his grip and allow you to take the juji Gatame.

Head punch

Punch the opponent in the face, when the pain hits, the opponent will release his grip and allow you to take the juji Gatame.

Arm Bars and Locks

Chapter Seven

Drilling

Drilling is the bread and butter training of everyone that I ever knew or read about that was any good. The more you drill the more the technique becomes yours, once you acquire the 'feel' the technique will be yours forever. It's not as if you have to drill these techniques for ever more (though there will always be new ones to drill) but you do have to in the beginning.

When I was first learning and perfecting my hand techniques I would think nothing of going for a 5 mile run and then doing any thing up to 40 rounds on the punch bag to get my hands where I wanted them to be. Sometimes my hands and arms would hurt so much that I couldn't hit at all on my seminars. My friends said that I was mad and that 40 rounds in one session was, at best, unhealthy, and of course there were the sceptics that didn't believe I did 40 rounds any way.

But there were things that I found in those marathon sessions that could not be discovered in any other way (how much your hands hurt for one thing), intangible things, a certain 'feel' for a technique, a new discovery. Things that have stayed with me to this day and will forever more, things that I cannot even pass on to my own students because I can't explain them properly. But when people look at my technique they see and feel something there that they do not see and feel in their own technique or the technique of other people.

When they ask me what that extra something is I cannot give them the answer, only that I found the intangible difference in one of my marathon sessions. When I went to Bob Spour to learn the ferocious art of Thai he couldn't believe how quick I picked it up. I picked up the technique because I would take it away with me and treat it like a day at work (not that I encourage conventional work of course, far better to spend your days training, or talking about training, or reading about training, or watching videos about training), I would spend whole sessions on the right leg thigh kick, then whole sessions on the left leg. I spent hours and hours and hours just on single technique, and it is the most boring thing to do, but in one month you can put in more flight time than another person will get in two years. Then people say to you 'you got your instructors certificate quick didn't you?' As though it was given to you free with the lid of a cornflakes packet, and I'd reply 'yea, while you were in the pub talking about it I was in the gym doing it'. Hence the expression 'the Thai leg kick? Yea, I spent five years on that one night!' So drilling is important, and the more the better, very few people have the discipline to isolate a technique and work it for hours on end, if you do then that will make you different and put you to the top of the class.

I will list an assortment of drills that I actually practice, but bear in mind that these are not cast in stone, change them, make up your own, do what ever you like as long as it allows you to repeat the moves over and over until they become a part of you and if the going gets a little tough and you feel like giving up remember, if it was easy everyone would be good.

From the mount
Juji Gatame(arm bar)
Sit through to your right and take the full Juji gatame, sit back into the mount and do the same to the left hand side-25 reps each side.

Reverse arm bar
Take the arm bar from the mount position only this time get the opponent to roll onto his belly, as though trying to escape. When he does employ the reverse arm bar return to the mount and do the same to the opposite side-25 reps each side.

Standing arm bar to Juji Gatame
From reverse arm bar position have the opponent stand up as though trying to escape, as he stands employ the standing arm bar. When the opponent

taps force him over onto his back and make a seated Juji Gatame, then back to the start position. Repeat 25 times to the left and then change and do 25 reps to the right.

From Scarf Hold
Five bar and lock drill

As in the chapter on bars from the scarf hold position go through the five bars and tie offs in quick succession. Push his right arm, at the elbow and palm up, across your right thigh. Switch legs to create a higher fulcrum by bringing your left leg through and pushing your right leg back and bar the arm over your left leg-quickly switch back your legs and drive his arm, at the elbow joint, into/over the lower fulcrum of your right leg-tie his arm off under your reverse/left leg-then to finish tie the arm off under your right leg. Do this sequence 25 times and the do the same on the other side of the opponent from a left scarf hold.

Ground Fighting: Volume Four

Juji Gatame

Sit through and make the bar, then straight back to the scarf hold position-repeat for 25 reps and then change to the left scarf hold and repeat the sequence.

From Upper 4 1/4 Juji Gatame

Take the bar from the upper 4 1/4 and then go straight back to the start position and repeat for 25 reps-both sides.

These are just a few to keep you going, I could fill the whole book with drills but there would be no sense in that so, make your own up and practice until your sick to death of the technique-then you'll be good at it.

Arm Bars and Locks

Conclusion

I hope that this book has given you the taste for the bars and lock. Remember, stick with them they are not near as immediate as the chokes and strangles but, once perfected they certainly are as effective and they definitely do work when the shit hits the fan and reality is on the menu. My friend Neil Adams won the world Judo championships, one of the toughest fighting arenas on the planet, against a Japanese opponent, with Juji Gatame so, if you can work it against one of the top Judoka in the world, some one that has developed the manipulative strength and knowledge to block the technique then you will make it work against just about anyone.

Ground Fighting: Volume Four

Many people give up on the Kansetsu-Waza because they seem over technical and take a lot of learning, after failing once or twice they throw them away, please don't be one of those people, stick with it, persevere, study and you'll enjoy one of the most devastating finishing techniques in any arena that there is to have. There will be more on arm bars and chokes in the last two volumes of this series Vol 6- Fighting From Your Back and Vol 5-Fighting From Your Knees.

Thank you very much for taking the time to read this text, I hope it has helped, and I hope that you enjoy the rest of the series.

Real Self Defence

Geoff Thompson

This complete illustrated manual includes a full range of techniques together with advice on awareness and avoidance of threat, fear control, weapons, law, and adrenalin switches. Also included are enlightening interviews with convicted muggers and their victims.

235 x 156 mm 176 pp ISBN 1 873475 16 0
£12.99 Paperback

Real Grappling

Geoff Thompson

Grappling is probably the oldest genre of combat known to man. This extensively illustrated manual takes you step by step through all the moves and techniques needed to become competent in the grappling arts.

235 x 156 mm 176 pp ISBN 1 873475 21 7
£12.99 Paperback

Real Punching

Geoff Thompson

Learn to pack a powerful punch with this illustrated manual that includes all the necessary moves and techniques to become competent in the punching arts.

235 x 156 mm 176 pp ISBN 1 873475 26 8
£12.99 Paperback

The Pavement Arena

Adapting Combat Martial Arts to the Street

Geoff Thompson

This illustrated manual takes the martial artist step by step through everything necessary to convert their skills for use in the 'street'.

235 x 156 mm 128 pp ISBN 1 873475 11 X
£9.95 Paperback

Real Kicking

Geoff Thompson

The realities of kicking in the street scenario are unveiled once and for all in this concise, professional, and down-to-earth book. All the moves and techniques needed to become competent in the kicking arts are included in this illustrated manual.

235 x 156 mm 176 pp ISBN 1 873475 31 4
£12.99 Paperback

Real Head, Knees and Elbows

Geoff Thompson

The final book in the **REAL** series, this volume includes devastating head, knee and elbow techniques from every range.

235 x 156 mm 176 pp ISBN 1 873475 77 2
£12.99 Paperback **September 1996**

Weight Training for the Martial Artist

Geoff Thompson

This illustrated book shows the routines that helped Geoff become one of the world's leading martial artists. Whatever your art there is a routine in this book that will give you the muscular armour to place you a cut above the rest.

245 x 190 mm 104 pp ISBN 1 873475 13 6
£9.99 Paperback

Animal Day

Pressure Testing the Martial Arts

Geoff Thompson

Animal Day explores the myths about what does and does not work on violent streets. The reader is educated in all aspects of pressure testing the martial arts to ensure that character and technique are not lacking when a situation becomes 'live'. As seen on Channel 4's **Passengers**, **Loaded** Magazine, **Maxim** Magazine, **MAI** Magazine etc

245 x 190 mm 102 pp ISBN 1 873475 18 7
£9.99 Paperback

On The Door

Further Bouncer Adventures

Geoff Thompson

new

The violence is graphic, the stories insightful and the laughs are plentiful as Geoff recalls four years on the door at a notorious establishment where violence was the norm.

216 x 135 mm 192 pp
ISBN 1 873475 72 1
£12.99 Hardback **September 1996**

Bouncer

Geoff Thompson

Sequel to **Watch My Back**, with more witty and violent bouncer stories. Geoff recounts his experiences with compelling wit and irony.

"Everyone in the country should read Geoff's work: it's both powerful and disturbing."
BBC Radio 4

216 x 135 mm 208 pp
ISBN 1 873475 04 7
£14.99 Hardback

Watch My Back

A Bouncer's Story

Geoff Thompson

The original cult classic. A story of mental and physical triumph over adversity at the front line of some of the world's roughest clubs.

"Anyone wishing to overcome their fears of violence and life must read this book."
Muscle Magazine

As seen on BBC1, ITV, Channel 4, SKY, Radio 1 & Radio 4.

216 x 135 mm 176 pp
ISBN 1 873475 03 9
£12.99 Hardback

KARATE BOXING KICK BOXING GRAPPLING
COMPETITION TRAINING IT'S ALL AT

COMBAT GYM

COVENTRY

Open Monday to Friday 9am -10 pm
Saturday & Sunday 10am - 3pm

For Information on classes
Tel: 01203 676287

PRIVATE TUITION AVAILABLE

ask about our
OPEN COMPETITION CLASS
Proprietors: Ian McCranor & Jim Burns

COMBAT GYM
WINSFORD AVENUE
ALLESLEY PARK COVENTRY